CW00672856

Vincent Strudwick

IS THE ANGLICAN CHURCH CATHOLIC?

The Catholicity of Anglicanism

DARTON·LONGMAN+TODD

© 1994 Vincent Strudwick

Published by Darton, Longman and Todd, 1 Spencer Court, 140–142 Wandsworth High Street, London SW18 4JJ in association with Affirming Catholicism, St Mary-le-Bow, Cheapside, London EC2V 6AU

ISBN 0–232–52095-X

The views expressed in this booklet are those of the author and do not necessarily reflect any policy of Affirming Catholicism

Booklets designed by Bet Ayer, phototypeset by Intype, London and printed by Halstan and Co Ltd, Amersham, Bucks

CONTENTS

Towards an Anglican Understanding of the Church   1

Introduction   1
The break with Rome   2
Mystical and visible   4
Nineteenth-century developments   6
Dispersed authority   8

Catholicity and Authority   11
Under *authority*   11
Anglican collegiality   12
Provisional structures   14

Catholicity and the Ordination of Women to the Priesthood   16
Unilaterally out of order?   16
An act of eschatological obedience   17
An ecumenical agenda   20

Catholicity and Ecumenism: from Jerusalem to Porvoo   22
A Catholic Anglican development?   22
The Porvoo Agenda   24

Notes   26

Affirming Catholicism

Affirming Catholicism has never been, and is not intended to be, yet another 'party' within the Church of England, or the Anglican Communion but rather a movement of encouragement and hope.

A group of lay people and clergy met together in 1990 to identify that authentic Catholic tradition within the Church which appeared to be under threat. Wider support was expressed at a public meeting on 9 June 1990 in London and at a residential conference in York in July 1991.

Since then Affirming Catholicism has been afforded charitable status. The following statement is extracted from the Trust Deed:

> It is the conviction of many that a respect for scholarship and free enquiry has been characteristic of the Church of England and of the Churches of the wider Anglican Communion from earliest times and is fully consistent with the status of those Churches as part of the Holy Catholic Church. It is desired to establish a charitable educational foundation which will be true both to those characteristics and to the Catholic tradition within Anglicanism ... The object of the foundation shall be the advancement of education in the doctrines and the historical development of the Church of England and the Churches of the wider Anglican Communion, as held by those professing to stand within the Catholic tradition.

In furtherance of these aims and objectives, Affirming Catholicism is producing this series of booklets. The series will encompass two sets of books: one set will attempt to present a clear, well-argued Catholic viewpoint on issues of debate facing the Church at any given time; the other set will cover traditional doctrinal themes. The editor of the series is Jeffrey John; the first four titles in the series were: *Imagining Jesus – An Introduction to the Incarnation* by Lewis Ayres; *Why Women Priests – The Ordination of Women and the Apostolic Ministry* by Jonathan Sedgwick; *History, Tradition and Change – Church History and the Development of Doctrine* by Peter Hinchcliff; *'Permanent, Faithful, Stable' – Christian Same-sex Partnerships* by Jeffrey John. Other titles are: *Christ in Ten Thousand Places – A Catholic Perspective on Christian Encounter with Other Faiths* by Michael Ipgrave; *Politics and the Faith Today – Catholic Social Vision for the 1990s* by Kenneth Leech; *Making Present – The Practice of Catholic Life and Liturgy* by Christopher Irvine; *Lay Presidency at the Eucharist?* by H. Benedict Green.

To order these publications individually or on subscription, or for enquiries regarding the aims and services of Affirming Catholicism write to:

The Secretary
Mainstream
St Mary-le-Bow
Cheapside
London EC2V 6AU

Tel: 071–329–3070

Towards an Anglican Understanding
of the Church

Introduction

'I esteem the Church of England the best Church of the Christian World, and think my time very well employed (whatever thanks I meet with for it) in defending its cause, and preserving persons in the communion of it.'[1] So wrote the seventeenth-century theologian Edward Stillingfleet, and while it may seem contentious to begin a paper on the catholicity of the Church by such a partisan statement, it is surely important that those who would explore the catholicity of the Church of England and the Anglican Communion should do so from a position of (not uncritical) appreciation of their Church and its history, its people and its contemporary mission.

Inevitably the title and timing of this paper, following the decision of the General Synod of the Church of England in November 1992 in favour of the ordination of women to the priesthood, are conditioned by the perception expressed during the debate and since, that by taking this decision the Church of England is denying the claim that it is 'part of the one, holy, Catholic and apostolic Church'. According to David Silk, then Archdeacon of Leicester, the motion before Synod invited a Provincial Synod, without warrant in either Scripture or tradition, to act as though it were an Ecumenical Council;[2] for it was an action affecting the faith and order of the Church. In other words, catholicity is something we have had and which, by the decision of Synod and what follows, we shall henceforth lose.

'On what grounds do you stand, O presbyter of the Church of England?' Newman asked this question in the first of the *Tracts for the Times* in 1833 – a perceived time of crisis. Today those who have stood in the tradition of the Tractarians representing a theology that is Catholic but not Roman, expressed through a liturgical tradition rooted in the early Church and led by representatives of the historic episcopate, are being asked that question again.

Nowhere is there a satisfactory definition of 'Catholic' or 'catholicity', but we need a point of departure. Henri de Lubac writes: ' "Catholic" suggests the idea ... of a reality which is not scattered but on the contrary turned towards a centre which assures its unity, whatever the expanse in area or the internal differentiation might be'.[3] The Anglican Church is 'turned towards a centre' through its historic formularies and structures and its liturgical tradition. But the story is still unfolding. The Anglican Reformers focused on Patristic theology, as expressing an organic rather than a systematic way of understanding Scripture and the development of the tradition. Out of this emerged a distinctive ecclesiology which includes a particular way of understanding and exercising authority, and a ministerial priesthood which emerges from, and is the servant of, the whole people of God.

I hope to show that the Church of England, and subsequently the Anglican Communion, has explored various and differing understandings of the Church which perceive catholicity not as something that has been 'lost' – a charge levelled at the Church of England from time to time since the sixteenth century – but rather as something that all Christians have sought and have not yet attained. As William Temple is credited as saying, 'I believe in the holy catholic Church and sincerely regret that it does not at present exist.' More positively, it is catholicity as quest.

The Church of England emerged as a result of a rejection of the authority of Rome and, having so emerged, it found in its exploration of Scripture and tradition an ecclesiology that affirmed the idea of catholicity while acknowledging the realities of division.

To say that the November 1992 vote in the General Synod of the Church of England, and indeed the preceding votes in other Provincial Synods of the Anglican Communion, were *merely* acts of Provincial Synods on matters for which they had no authority to legislate is to misunderstand the historical reality of Anglicanism; for provincial autonomy is built into its very foundation and, as I hope to show, is integral to its understanding of the nature of catholicity.

The break with Rome

From its birth in the reign of Henry VIII the Church of England has held a variety of understandings of the nature of the Church and they have included the conviction that the Church of England is a part of the one holy, Catholic and apostolic Church. But how?

The changes through which this conviction was maintained, interpreted and developed included both the break with Rome and the change of allegiance associated with the reign of Henry VIII, as well as a re-formation of the Church during the reigns of Edward VI and Elizabeth I. The change in allegiance was undertaken by the King through Parliament between 1534 and 1545. It involved a recognition of the Monarch as being the source of authority for all matters – spiritual as well as temporal – and while on issues of faith and order Henry himself was very conservative and consistently wary of change, the Act of Supremacy in 1534 explicitly gave the King power to reform errors in doctrine. 'Our said sovereign Lord, his heirs and successors kings of his realm, shall have full power and authority from time to time to visit, repress, redress, reform, correct, restrain and amend all such errors, heresies, abuses, offences, contempts and enormities whatsoever they be . . .'[4]

In Elizabeth's reign, as theologians wrestled with the implications of what had happened, 'the supreme governorship' became a shared function between the Queen and Parliament. Already there was a tendency to play down the monarch's authority in doctrine 'by setting it in the context of the role of Parliament as the lay synod of the Church'.[5] This was opposed by the Queen, but the seed was there and flowered from 1644 to 1646 with the Westminster Assembly. Already the perception that the teaching of the *magisterium* needed to be received by the faithful to be truly authoritative was finding its way into the structures. However, neither this independence of jurisdiction nor the associated ability to change doctrine and order seems to have shifted the perception that there was 'one holy, Catholic Church'.

In the King's Book (1543), this one holy, Catholic Church is described as 'an assembly of people called out from one another as from infidels and heathens to one faith and confession in the name of Christ'. It is Catholic by its geography, for it teaches one faith, one truth and one baptism throughout the world, and in all places distributes God's word and sacraments – 'Pope or no Pope'. It is also Catholic by its continuity with the past, looking to the first four Councils as containing the essence of that teaching that derives from Scripture and is the basis of the Church's life. But as the break with Rome became established, it was important to determine the relationship between the mystical body and the Church militant. The Roman Catholic Church explicitly, from the Council of Trent onwards, claimed that the mystery of the Church is *ipso facto* the Roman Catholic Church. Even the Second Vatican Council says, 'The visible community [of the Church] and the mystical body of Christ are not two things but one reality, integrated from a human and a divine element . . . This Church, grounded in the world and ordered as a community, is the *Ecclesia Catholica* governed by the Pope and the bishops in union with him.'[6] On this view, the Church's catholicity can only be measured by reference to the Holy See. The die was cast by the mid-sixteenth century in this respect, for despite the efforts of Pole, Contarini and the group that had drawn up the programme for the reform of the Church in the 1530s, invitations to the Ecumenical Council were not sent to those Churches that had broken away from Rome. They were regarded as no longer members of the Catholic Church and therefore not entitled to be present.

There was a good deal of ambiguity in England due to the evident brokenness of the Church. In the Articles of Religion, Article XIX, *Of the Church*, never mentions the invisible Church; but it does not deny it. It teaches that 'The visible Church of Christ is a congregation of faithful men in which the pure Word of God is preached, and the sacraments be duly ministered according to Christ's ordinance in all those things that of necessity are requisite to the same.' During and indeed after the reign of Edward VI there was a strong influence from the Continent on the development of Anglican thinking about the nature of the Church. Hooper, who had lived in Zürich between 1547 and 1549, was made Bishop of Gloucester and wrote, 'I believe that the Lord God has given us three principal signs or marks by which we may know this his Church, that is to say, the Word, the Sacraments, and discipline.'[7] All the English Reformers seem to be agreed that the primary mark of the true Church is the Word of God evident in its life and preaching, and in this they are in agreement with the Continental Reformers. At this time they are still concerned with the visible Church; but as it becomes apparent that the split is not going to be healed, Anglican theologians have to come to grips with the relationship between a 'broken' visible Church and the mystical body. Thus Bishop Jewel, Bishop of Salisbury from 1560 and an important early apologist for Anglican claims, writes, 'The general or outward Church of God's elect is visible and may be seen; but the very true Church of God's elect is invisible and cannot be seen or discerned by man, but is known to God alone.'[8]

Mystical and visible
Richard Hooker, the apologist *par excellence* of the Elizabethan Settlement, was able to go further. He acknowledged that, 'For lack of diligent observing the difference first between the Church of God mystical and visible, then between the visible sound and corrupted, sometimes more, sometimes less, the oversights are neither few nor light, that are committed.'[9]

As far as the Church visible was concerned, Hooker could acknowledge that the Church of England was only *part* of the Catholic Church and existing for the preservation of Christianity in 'which consideration as the main body of the sea being one, yet within divers precincts has divers names; so the Catholic Church is in like sort divided into a number of distinct societies, every one of which is termed a church within itself'.[10] He could acknowledge that the Church of England itself was not without fault, and at the same time in some sense in fellowship with that part of the Roman Church which shared a common heritage and common concerns.

> We have held and do hold fellowship with them [i.e. Roman Catholics] for even as the Apostle doth say of Israel, that they are in one respect enemies but in another beloved of God; in like sort with Rome we dare not communicate concerning her gross and grievous abominations, yet touching those main parts of Christian truth wherein they constantly still persist, we gladly acknowledge them to be of the family of Jesus Christ.[11]

The Church was for Hooker an organic, not static, institution and what the New Testament envisages in its imagery of the Church is to some extent present in the visible Church, but imperfectly. The mystery is present but incompletely revealed. The catholicity of the Church, then, is found by those who are attentive to the Gospel and its message and are attempting to be formed in the image of the Church of which it speaks. This formation is 'the tradition' which with Scripture and reason forms a 'threefold cord, not quickly broken'. Catholicity is experienced in the dynamic of this threefold cord, in communion – albeit impaired – with the visible Church in other places, and by the way in which, through its local expression in life and worship, it bears the marks of the Gospel.

For Hooker, much of the way we represent the Gospel and the forms through which we do this have to be framed with regard to the 'place and the persons for which they are made'. 'Seeing that nations are not all alike, surely the giving of one kind of positive laws unto one only people, without any liberty to alter them, is but slender proof, that therefore one kind should in like sort be given to serve everlastingly for all.'[12] Church order is what is *expedient*, and moreover we have the authority to change it. To this we shall return.

We note a refusal to sacrifice the doctrine of the visible Church for the invisible and vice versa, which persisted through the seventeenth century. The Church of England held both concepts together, realising the impossibility of stating exhaustively the relations between the invisible Church of the Holy Ones and the visible Church with its continuous tradition of creeds and sacraments, scriptures and ministry. Further, though the Church of England continued to enhance the value of the visible Church and her means of grace, she had no intention of underrating the doctrine of the invisible Church.

Here we have it: that our present catholicity lies in the *invisible* Church, and to the reality of this invisible or mystical Church we all aspire but do not in this present age attain. Both Anglican and Roman Catholic were in many ways quite similar. They recognised one Church and that this was Catholic as well as holy and apostolic. Each claimed to present itself as the one that came nearest to this ideal, whereas in the other only vestiges of Christianity remained. Each accused the other of introducing novelties. But certainly the Church of England was conscious of its own deficiencies as well. It took a little longer for the Roman Catholic Church to acknowledge this, but it did so in the Second Vatican Council when it stated, 'This empirical Church reveals the mystery [of the Church] but *not without shadows*, and it does so until it is brought into the full light of Christ, who also reached glory through humiliation.'

Vatican II was able to state with admirable clarity what the Church of England tried to state much less clearly in the sixteenth century, that the New Testament envisages the mystery of the Church as present in the empirical Church but under all kinds of historical veils and distortions: the mystery is present but incompletely revealed. It was surely on this that T. S. Eliot was reflecting when he wrote his poem about the hippopotamus being taken up to join the Church Triumphant, where:

> He shall be washed as white as snow,
> By all the virgin martyrs kist,
> While the True Church remains below
> Wrapt in the old miasmal mist.[13]

At the heart of the various Anglican understandings of its catholicity is the perception that the universality of the visible Church is impaired because the communion is incomplete, but that in its local expression the Catholic Church is 'there'. However, the qualitative wholeness of that local expression is also impaired, for no expression of the Catholic Church is ever 'without shadows', until the *eschaton*, when they will be identical.

I have dwelt on the origins of the Church of England's ecclesiology in the sixteenth century partly because this has been obscured by later historical 'myths', and partly because it was from these roots that an Anglican ecclesiology developed, when the Communion began to grow in the nineteenth century. What I have described underlines the break with Rome and shows a distinct development in the way Canterbury and Rome understood the nature of the Church and their relationship with each other. But there also emerged a strong desire to show that the Church of England was *the* true heir of the Catholic Church in this country. Diarmaid MacCulloch has written:

> The myth was created in two stages, first in the middle years of the seventeenth century and then from the third decade of the nineteenth century – in either case by a 'High Church' party within the Church: first the Laudians or Arminians, later the Tractarians or Anglo-Catholics. These parties consisted largely of clergy with the particular motive of emphasising the structural Catholic continuity of the Church over the break of the Reformation in order to claim that the true representative of the Catholic Church within the borders of England and Wales was not the minority loyal to the bishop of Rome but the Church as by law established in 1559 and 1662.[14]

For them, the Catholic Church in England was the Church of England.

The heirs of this tradition focused on the faith delivered to the saints through Scripture and the first four Councils, the continuity of the Church of England with its medieval predecessor, the Church's authority and unity expressed through the historic episcopate and the sacramental life mediated through a ministerial priesthood. Rome was seen as an intrusive rival.

Nineteenth-century developments
In the massive intellectual and social changes of the nineteenth century, with Erastian pressures threatening the Church of England, a closer definition of its catholicity was called for. For Newman, the catholicity of the Church had

rested on the distinction between the invisible 'one, living and spiritual' and the visible community of the Church, which is 'a guide to what is inward, sometimes visible; a guide to what is spiritual'. The ecclesial community is:

> that great invisible company who are one and all incorporated in the one mystical Body of Christ and quickened by one Spirit . . . The visible ministry on earth, the Bishops and Pastors, together with Christians depending on them, at this or that day is *called* the Church, though really but a fragment of it, as being that part of it which is seen and can be pointed out and as resembling it in type, and witnessing it, and *leading towards it* [my italics].[15]

In this, Newman shows himself an heir of Hooker.[16]

The state of the Anglican episcopate at the time, however, caused Newman much anxiety. The visible part expressed through the Church of England, in his view was so *much* in shadow that he found it difficult to believe it had company with the real thing – the mystical body. Some responded to his criticism by trying to set out more clearly the structural position of the Church of England in relation to the Church universal and visible. One such was William Palmer, a Fellow of Worcester College, Oxford, described by the Jesuit Perrone as '*theologorum Oxoniensium facile princeps*'. In his *Treatise on the Church of Christ*[17] he expounded what he conceived to be the Anglican doctrine of the Church in the so-called 'branch' theory. Baldly this states that though the Church may have fallen into schism, each part of it – Roman, Eastern and Anglican – may yet be a 'branch' of the one Church of Christ, provided it holds the original faith of the undivided Church and maintains the apostolic succession of its bishops. The 'branch' theory *limits* the 'Catholic Church' to three branches, and Catholic Anglicans in the past hundred years have frequently dwelt on the special relationship that this implies. However, Roman Catholics, and also some Anglicans such as A. M. Ramsey, have found it unsatisfactory.

The structural line of thinking of this theory has a concern for maintaining the Faith and Order of the Church as inherited, and it has given rise to a great anxiety among Anglicans about the credentials for the validity of their orders, and a concern that these should be accepted by the Roman Catholic Church. This concern seems to be vindicated by John Jay Hughes, ordained an Anglican priest but not subsequently re-ordained when he became a priest in the Roman Church. He has argued that both in terms of 'intention' and of the technicality of the succession, Anglican orders are valid.[18] However, the resulting correspondence in *The Tablet* showed how little the acceptance of the technical succession counted in the eyes of a large number of Roman Catholics, for they perceived that what was at issue was not a technicality but an understanding of *ecclesia*. If you are schismatic and heretical, what value can be given to an impeccable tactile apostolic succession?

For Newman, in the years after 1838, the edges between the visible and invisible ecclesial community become increasingly blurred and he admits that the Church, for him, is 'like a building seen through a mist'.[19] As this happened, so he became less able to deal with the reality of the Church of England, especially when in his perception it was engaged in a process which was heretical and inimical to the Faith. In 1841 a bishopric was set up in Jerusalem to serve the Anglicans and Protestants of the Middle East. The scheme envisaged that the bishop was to be nominated by England and Prussia alternately and was a tacit union between the Church of England and a Lutheran Church without guarantees for the preservation of Church Order or Doctrine. To many, it appeared to be a sign that the Church of England was prepared to sacrifice Catholic principle for political expediency, and in the controversy Newman came to compare the Church of England to an empire breaking up, a kingdom shattered into fragments. Yet at this stage he still held out the prospects of a new community which would one day shine out, led by great bishops of the Church in the tradition of Cyprian, Basil, Ambrose and Leo. He pleads, 'If we claim to *be* the Church, let us act the Church and we shall *become* the Church'. It was almost his last Anglican breath. For Newman it was the perception that civil authorities could impose their will on national churches and put at risk their Catholic purity that drew him to Rome, 'because I think the Church of Rome the Catholic Church, and ours not a part of the Catholic Church *because not in communion with Rome* [my italics].'[20]

The specifically Anglican pilgrimage towards catholicity was pursued by those who remained – while the Roman Catholic Church, itself not exempt from the pressures towards nationalism, was profoundly transformed. 'Between 1850 and 1900, the Roman Catholic Church was changed from a loose federation of churches with the Pope in the chair into the modern rigid bureaucratic organisation with a common culture that had to include all the Catholics.'[21] For Fr André Lascaris OP, to whom I owe that quotation, the concept of a Christian Europe was born in the nineteenth century, but it was born in the name of the myth of the Catholic Middle Ages and in the process all the remaining structures of the medieval Church were destroyed. What Newman had joined was destroyed by the revolutions and a much more rigid and authoritarian system emerged.

Dispersed authority
While the Roman Catholic Church was compelled to opt for a centralised authority, the Anglican Communion, on the basis of its own history and Church polity, felt its way towards an understanding and exercise of what became known as 'dispersed authority'.[22] This was pioneered in the nineteenth century by three successive archbishops, Longley, Tait and Benson. A Synod of the Anglican Church in Canada in 1865 called for some sort of

Council to define doctrine, to which idea there was strenuous opposition. But out of it came the ten-yearly Lambeth Conferences, which were conceived as 'brotherly consultations'. The first Conference in 1867 issued a statement which began, 'We, Bishops of Christ's Holy Catholic Church, in visible communion with the Church of England and Ireland, professing the faith delivered to us in holy scriptures, maintained by the primitive Church and by the Fathers of the English Reformation, summed up in the Creeds, affirmed by the undisputed General Councils . . .'[23] Here were their credentials for catholicity; the challenge was how to make them work for catholicity. Perhaps the most important thinker in this respect was Archbishop Benson. Mark Chapman says of his vision of unity:

> In Benson's judgement a conception emerges of the unity which cannot be imposed by a foreign authority but arises in response to the organic need to find an outward and visible expression for the ultimate unity of Christ: the Church exists as a sacramental witness to the unity of Christ. Consequently unity was not merely a spiritual matter, but carried outward the visible signs . . . The visibility of unity in the episcopacy, however, did not exist solely in virtue of a supernatural succession from the Apostles, but in its protection of the truth delivered through the Apostles, which found its origin and would yet find its goal in Christ. Where such truth found no protection, there the line of succession was broken.[24]

Here indeed is a catholicity which is related to the sixteenth-century concern that the primary mark of the true Church is the Word of God, a mark which illuminates the real meaning of the apostolic succession.

The development of this understanding of the nature of Anglican catholicity was both inevitable and necessary, as the formative role of the Church of England in developing Anglicanism has given way to worldwide partnership, some of which predates the British Empire and which today is no longer co-extensive with the Commonwealth. Chapman illustrates how Benson, Lock (a contributor to *Lux Mundi*) and William Temple 'each envisioned a Catholic unity in which Catholic meant, not a monolithic centralism, but the consecration of everything in human culture, in its huge diversity, to the service of Christ, in the constant quest for the full realisation of the truth'. Furthermore, Hooker's insistence that the form of the Church may vary according to local culture was reflected at the Lambeth Conference of 1908, when it affirmed that 'all races and peoples, whatever their language or conditions, must be welded into one body'; the communion must express unity in diversity. The developments in the Roman Catholic Church which have been described have enabled it to pronounce on matters of faith and order, and the doctrines of the Immaculate Conception and of the Infallibility of the Pope are two examples. There has been continuing separate development of the two Churches, so that we are now not just talking about issues that were of concern at the time of the Reformation, but also about four hundred years of separate ecclesial development. The fact that this is more remarkable for its convergence than for its differences is something for which we must give thanks, but where there are differences, it is at present difficult for the Roman Catholic Church to consider anything other than ways by which these differences may be conformed to Roman Catholic teaching – because in its view the mystical Body and the visible Church are one. If, however, we hold an Anglican ecclesiology which distinguishes between these two, then the insights of both churches and of other traditions may be brought into the conversation as we together seek to determine the faith which is at the basis of catholicity in the mystical Body.

However, the issues of the nineteenth century raise sharply the question of how, without a Pope, the diversity of the Anglican communion could in any sense be 'welded into one body', and raise questions also about what authority can properly be exercised in determining how the eternal Gospel should be proclaimed and in what Order.

Catholicity and Authority

Under authority
' "Off with her head," said the Red Queen. Nobody moved.'[25] As Lewis Carroll well knew, there is a difference between being authoritarian and being authoritative, although they are often confused. If the Church is to be Catholic, it requires authority, but because of the nature of its goals it requires authority of a particular kind, whose exercise is discernibly in tune with those goals. In many, if not most, of its cultural manifestations, the authority it has modelled has not seemed to be consistent with its goals. With its own peculiar understanding of the Church, has Anglicanism a contribution to make?

In the Catholic tradition throughout the Christian world, authority has been exercised through bishops. The bishop's authority is first of all based on conformity to the Gospel – he, or she, like the centurion in St Luke's Gospel (Luke 7:1–10), is one '*under* authority', and has the responsibility for *diacrisis* or discernment, that is, discerning what Christ is saying to the Church and declaring it with authority. The bishop is in effect the unifier of the Church, not by minimising or abolishing conflict, but through a ministry which attempts to show the face of Christ to those who are struggling with differing understandings of truth and discipleship.

In the Eastern Orthodox tradition, catholicity is expressed in the *local* and the responsibility for policy-making in the Christian community is the local bishop's. The bishop in turn has to be recognised by other bishops in the episcopate and their mutual recognition of each other is sufficient authority for maintaining catholicity. The Orthodox tradition has felt less need for structures than any other Christian body – but episcopacy is for them, as throughout the Church, a system through which the Church performs its task. During its history, the system has gone through changes so radical that 'change' is too soft a word to describe them. Perhaps mutation is better. Mutation is a biological process of change which results from time to time in a new species. In mutation there are elements both of continuity and of discontinuity and I believe this is what has happened in the evolution of episcopacy. However, in spite of the changing forms of the system, which are related to historical development and social and cultural change, the primary functions of the bishop are the same, and these are to deliver the Gospel (the apostolic task) and to ensure the care and growth of those who receive it (the ministerial or diaconal task). The essence of the Anglican episcopal system lies in the relationship between the bishop and the local church, focused through the Incumbent and acknowledged in the induction service, where his responsibilities are set out and delivered with the words: 'Receive this cure of souls, which is both yours and mine.'

Episcopacy has been challenged in its different manifestations throughout Church history. It has most of all been challenged when it has not honoured this fundamental relationship. In the seventeenth century Richard Baxter, noted for his opposition to prelacy, would have been much more contented if there had been *more* bishops. If bishops were people who focused and resourced mission and ministry for the local church, then they were to be respected. It was because they did not appear to be able to do this, as the system became detached from the Church's task, that he objected to episcopacy in its current form and later rejected the offer of the bishopric of Hereford, following the return of Charles II.

It was during the nineteenth century, following the economic and social changes of the Industrial Revolution, that the desire to make episcopal authority effective again drove people to pioneer a *synodical system* in order to renew the links between the bishop and the local church. The diocese of Oxford under Wilberforce and the diocese of Lincoln under Wordsworth explored the possibilities of Anglican synods in the teeth of opposition from those who feared that synods were signs of a new model of Church government. The reformers leant heavily on an interesting book published in 1748, *Concerning Diocesan Synods*, by Pope Benedict XIV. This was an attempt to understand the nature of a synod in the history of the Church and to apply its use to the new situation in the Roman Church. Benedict makes three points:

— All the clergy *must* be summoned.
— It is within the discretion of the bishop to invite the laity *ad consulendum*.
— In so far as legislation is concerned, the bishop is the sole legislator.

While this synodical aspect of episcopacy was slow to take root in England, it became increasingly important in the development of episcopacy and the exercise of authority in the various emerging Provinces of the Anglican Communion.

Anglican collegiality
But how is the authority of the local church exercised in relation to authority in other local churches? How is collegiality maintained?

For Roman Catholics, the Pope is said to be to the whole Church what the bishop is to the local community: that is, the interpreter of each to all and the focal point of unity. The Petrine office has been criticised in the past when people have perceived that the Pope has abused his responsibility, as in the sixteenth century; when the office has been magnified, as in the nineteenth century; or when it has been seen to be ineffectual, as in the seventeenth century. Edward Stillingfleet, whom I quoted at the beginning of this paper, has a passage in which he asks how decisions taken in Rome can possibly be effective in Mexico or Japan. What is plainly needed, he argues, is for decisions to be taken in those places where they can be put into practice at once. The speed of modern travel and the word processor and fax machine have made this argument less cogent than it was in 1664, and a glance at the pictures in *Osservatore Romano* week by week shows hundreds of bishops on *ad limina* visits to the Pope who, with amazing energy, attempts to keep in touch with every bishop in his Church.

Nevertheless, increasingly widespread disobedience to Catholic teaching raises the question of the effectiveness of the process of decision-making in such a structure, for in spite of the striking visibility of communication exemplified by the present Pope, the system *as it is* surely will not effectively serve the Catholic Church of the future. In fact the Pope sometimes looks like a rather popular Red Queen, for crowds turn out to cheer him but have no intention of obeying, say, the ruling on contraception.

In a review of Fr Aidan Nichols' book on the theological history of the Church of England,[26] Bishop Nazir Ali writes, 'Fr Nichols appears to believe that authority in the Church, if it is to be effective, must be infallible. But is this necessarily the case? Can the teachers in the Church not be regarded as authoritative interpreters of the Apostolic Faith, while admitting that they may sometimes err both individually and as a body, and have to be corrected by the very deposit of faith which they seek to interpret?'[27] It is indeed part of the essence of Anglican ecclesiology that every church has 'erred' and none is 'without shadows'. On this view, none can claim to be Catholic but all are bound to seek catholicity.

At the end of the last century, as I have described, the desire for some top level authoritative *praesidium* to determine matters of faith and order in the Church of England was abandoned in favour of the Lambeth Conference which concentrates upon the formation of general attitudes and perspectives. The concern has been to preserve a *consensus fidelium* and a collegiality of bishops. At the Lambeth Conference of 1988 great emphasis was laid on the concerns of the diocese being brought to Lambeth by the bishop. Similarly 'taking Lambeth back to the diocese' was regarded as essential to the whole process. While in the provinces of the Anglican Communion different models of 'Bishop in Synod' operate, all have been developed with checks and balances designed both to protect the bishop and the faithful from gross error, and also to ensure the catholicity of the Church through emerging and rather tentative structures which allow a *consensus fidelium* to be discerned.

Provisional structures

A report on the Inter-Anglican Theological Doctrinal Consultation states:

> Anglicans have become accustomed to speak of the dispersed authority exercised within the communion. Episcopal ministry is included in the bonds of interdependence but there is also an authority appropriate to clergy and laity engaged in the mission, worship and governance of the Church. We also note that authority is dispersed among the autonomous, self-governing Provinces of the Communion. There are three other sources of authority which overlap but are not co-terminous: the authority granted to Church leaders by election or appointment to office, the authority inherent in professional competence, and not least the authority of men and women who by prayer, loving relationships and reflection on daily experience have grown wise in holy living and exercise a profoundly prophetic role in the life of the Church.[28]

In all this, the Anglican Church has been developing a model of episcopal government which gives effect to the ideal of subsidiarity, with the participation of those spoken of as 'sources of authority' feeding through the bishop into the provincial structure of inter-episcopal relationships in the communion. That these are imperfect is acknowledged. Yet they are such as to allow new developments, including the ordination of women to the priesthood, to emerge, while seeking to maintain a dialogue with other members of the Universal Church. Catholic Anglicans do not rule out some concept of a changed papacy, as Archbishop Runcie acknowledged in his opening address to the Lambeth Conference of 1988:

> Anglicans have become accustomed to speak of a dispersed authority. And we are traditionally suspicious of the Lambeth Conference becoming anything other than a conference. We may indeed wish to discuss the development of more solid structures of unity and coherence. But I for one would want their provisional character made absolutely clear; like tents in the desert, they should be capable of being easily dismantled when it is time for the Pilgrim People to move on. We have no intention of developing an alternative papacy. We would rather continue to deal with the structures of the existing Petrine Ministry, and hopefully help in its continuing development and reform as a ministry of unity for all Christians.[29]

The Conference reinforced the four embodiments of unity: the Archbishop of Canterbury, the Lambeth Conference, the Anglican Consultative Council, and the Meeting of Primates. Through these, the Anglican Communion will continue to work at a provisional model for coherence and decision making while developing the dialogue with Rome over the nature of the Petrine ministry. It is through these 'embodiments' that the different decision making processes of the Provinces are shared and the results given coherence in the gradual and continuing development of attitudes and perspectives that will enable the Church to live and preach the Gospel most effectively.

ARCIC,[30] in wrestling with the issue of authority in the Church, emphasised the way in which the ministerial priesthood represents the people to God and Christ to the people. According to ARCIC, it is through this relationship that the *sensus fidelium* is interpreted and issues in authoritative statements at appropriate levels from the diocesan bishop to provincial councils presided over by an archbishop. ARCIC sees this structure inevitably crowned by some form of primacy, arguing that the 'Fathers and Doctors of the Church gradually came to interpret the New Testament data as pointing to [a Petrine primacy]'. Clearly many Anglicans are not going to assent to an infallible primacy, and Catholic Anglicans may press for a new model which takes account of their own experience of 'being under' authority.

Catholicity and the Ordination
of Women to the Priesthood

Unilaterally out of order?
The shocked disbelief of many Catholic Anglicans following the vote in Synod in November 1992, which opened the way to the ordination of women to the priesthood in the Church of England, focused in the question, 'By what authority has this been done?' John Selwyn Gummer, at the time Minister of Agriculture, Fisheries and Food and a member of the General Synod, wrote in *The Tablet* on 24 April 1993, 'By asserting that it can alter doctrine and order unilaterally, it has relinquished its apostolic claims to the allegiance of the people of England'. In his view a Church owning itself 'as only one part of the Body of Christ' can claim no power to change unilaterally what 'everywhere and always and by everyone has been believed'.

In writing this, Gummer first of all isolated the Church of England from a process that has been going on in the Anglican Communion for a very long time. In fact it is not only the General Synod of the Church of England that has seen fit to take this decision, but a large part of the Anglican Communion as a whole, and when the first priests were canonically and legitimately ordained in the United States, the position of the Church of England was already 'compromised' in the eyes of the Roman Catholic Church. Of course there was still the prominence and prestige of Canterbury, which gives the November vote a particular focus.

Secondly, this statement took no account of the Anglican ecclesiology and its traditions of the exercise of authority and ministry that we have outlined in this paper. In this Mr Gummer is not alone. The Roman Catholic Bishops' Conference of England and Wales, issuing its eirenic statement on 23 April 1993, nevertheless focuses the puzzlement of many Roman Catholics concerning the decision and the anguish of some Catholic Anglicans who had approached members of the Roman Catholic Bishops' Conference 'with the desire to find their way of living the Catholic faith in visible communion with the Holy See' as a result of Synod's decision. 'For many people [the decision to admit women to ordination to the priesthood] has given rise to serious questions about the kind of Christian authority claimed and exercised in the Church of England.'[31] This puzzlement – and indeed concern – was expressed by both the Pope and Cardinal Willibrands in correspondence with the Archbishop of Canterbury when the process began in the Anglican communion. From the point of view of the Roman Catholic Church and its understanding of the nature of the Church and the nature of authority, such a decision necessarily raises a further obstacle in the road towards unity. Pope Paul VI had said that contemplating this step introduced into the dialogue between Anglicans and Roman Catholics 'an element of grave difficulty'. In a letter to Archbishop Runcie dated 20 December 1984, Pope John Paul II used stronger language, describing it as 'a threat'. 'We have celebrated together the progress towards reconciliation between our two communions. But . . . the number of Anglican Churches which admit or are preparing to admit women to priestly ordination constitutes in the eyes of the Catholic Church an increasingly serious obstacle to their progress.'[32]

The significant document for Roman Catholics is *Inter insigniores* of October 1976. The argument is that while the New Testament does not consider the matter and therefore neither confirms nor forbids it, Jesus did not call women to the apostolate and in the spread of Christianity and the development of ministerial priesthood, in spite of the change of many customs, the ordination of women was not permitted except among certain heretical sects. While there is an equality of the baptised in the Church, that equality exists in a differentiated body in which men and women have roles which are not merely functional but are deeply rooted in Christian anthropology and sacramentology. Consequently, the Catholic Church feels unable to make the change.

As long ago as 1963, the Archbishops' Commission on Women and Holy Orders, appointed to make a thorough examination of the various reasons for 'the withholding of the ordained and representative priesthood from women', included an interesting third view by Alan Richardson, formerly Professor of Christian Theology at Nottingham University but then Dean of York, which argued that while it might be theologically correct to ordain women to the priesthood, it was inexpedient. 'In an age in which the possibilities of mutual understanding and of eventual reunion have been opened up before the eyes of Christians of many confessions, it would be inexpedient for any Church to embark upon unilateral action which would widen rather than heal the divisions within Christendom.'[33] That view seemed persuasive then, and for some the force of the argument has increased as events have unfolded.

An act of eschatological obedience

I believe, however, that this argument is outweighed by reference to the view of the Church that we have set out on our own model of reformed Catholicism. Under that ecclesiology all churches are fallible; their decisions may prove mistaken. However, through our own theological tradition involving the critical use of the Bible, the unfolding of the tradition, and allowing the insight of the Holy Spirit to open our eyes to new things that God may be saying, we are putting on to the agenda of the dialogue something that we believe to be important. This is an act of eschatological obedience to the future Catholic Church.

Robert Runcie wrote to the Pope in 1985: 'I would therefore propose to your Holiness the urgent need for a joint study of the question of the ordination of women to the priesthood, especially in respect of its consequences for the mutual reconciliation of our churches and the recognition of their ministries.'[34] As far as I know, there has been no reply to that suggestion, but it is on the agenda and that is an act of responsible intent. For it is not sufficient to have made a theological discovery and implemented it within its own structures. If we believe something to be true, it must be debated and represented throughout the broken body, as part of the process of healing. As Stephen Sykes has written,

> Doctrinal conflict may actually serve a constructive purpose in the Church so long as there is a tradition of communal worship, centrally authorised, in which the symbols and rituals of the Christian faith are openly spoken and performed, and the whole Christian community opened up to the interior dimension of the self-offering of Jesus. It is when this is being carried out that theologians may have the confidence to make the necessary experiments and to risk making the necessary mistakes.[35]

It is through theological debate and facing conflict that a *common* understanding of catholicity may be gained.

During the last decade, there has been a feeling in some quarters that the road to full communion might be swift. I do not think that has ever been the case. There are three dialogues taking place and they all help each other. There is the dialogue of smiles that has been going on since the Second Vatican Council. There is a dialogue of pastoral acknowledgement that often means there is a greater sharing and understanding of ministries at local level than has ever been before. There is also the dialogue of theological principle, which, because of the different nature of the structures of the Anglican and the Roman Catholic churches, is bound to take a very long time. Our commitment to catholicity requires us to take the unity of the Church with the greatest seriousness. The Eames Commission[36] spoke of the provisionality of an imperfect ministry in the present divided state of the Church; the provisionality of legislative decisions made where there is not a settled consensus; the provisionality of a ministry whose validity may subsequently be brought into question as development in the Church proceeds. But we have to recognise that our act of 'responsible intent' has produced a situation where there is no going back.

> In matters of faith, mistakes can be put right; in matters of order, such as the ordination of women to the priesthood and especially to the episcopate, the possib-

ility of subsequent rejection or alteration of a legislative decision raises peculiar difficulties, for an ordained woman is a fact, not a belief. If ordination is for life, as Anglicans believe, an ordained woman cannot be deemed to be ordained priest or consecrated bishop 'provisionally', even if the legislation which permits her ordination is itself deemed 'provisional'. A woman can hardly be ordained on the understanding that her ordination, and therefore the sacraments she administers, are in some way uncertain. Nor would it be easy to unravel the problems of ordinations by a woman bishop of priests (male or female) whose ordination is not recognised by some of their flock.[37]

While these difficulties cause apprehension and anxiety in the hierarchy, the fact of the ordination of women in the Anglican Communion has undoubtedly already moved the subject higher on the agenda of the Roman Catholic Church.[38] In the United States, for example, the Catholic Bishops' Committee on Women has opened an official dialogue with the Roman Catholic Women's Ordination Conference. Encouraged by the writings of Hans Küng and Edouard Schillebeeckx, among others, the movement has spread to many countries. In the *Catholic Herald* for 2 April 1993 we read that 'Catholic Women's Ordination, the first organisation in this country [England] aimed at achieving women's ordination in the Catholic Church, held the first of three scheduled "silent vigils of mourning for women's lost gifts" on the piazza of Westminster Cathedral.'[39] At a women's synod held in Milan in March 1993, 300 women discussed problems facing women in the Church, with the occasional presence of the Vicar General of the diocese. Douglas Brown SSM, of the Anglican Centre in Rome, tells of 'a meeting of eighteen theological professors in Barcelona, who have issued a report saying that there is no sufficiently weighty theological argument against the ordination of women, and that therefore there is a discrimination against women in the Church – and every act of discrimination is against the Gospel.'[40]

It is perhaps because of such thinking within the Roman Catholic Church that *Osservatore Romano* printed a series of articles in the spring of 1993 concerning the ordination of women. The Pontifical Biblical Commission, when first consulted on this subject, found no conclusive reasons against the ordination of women and recommended that there be further doctrinal studies of the subject. Albert Vanhoye, secretary of the Commission, Inos Biffi, of the Pontifical Faculty of Theology of Northern Italy, and Max Thurian, now a Roman Catholic but well known outside Catholic circles as a founder member of the community at Taizé, wrote key articles in a series which put the case for no change. Vanhoye argues that equality between men and women does not remove the differences in function which are shown in I Corinthians, while Biffi emphasises that the Church has refused to accept anthropological or cultural arguments for change in something which is accepted as a way of being faithful to Christ. Thurian argues that the ecclesial communities which accept the ordination of women to the ministry do not recognise a ministerial priesthood and that they thus ordain to a ministerial function rather than to a priestly state.

Such articles show that these writers have not really grasped the substance of the debate which has taken place in the Anglican Communion. In the Church of England's General Synod, no one put forward 'anthropological or cultural arguments'. The Evangelical concern for fidelity to Scripture ensured a rigorous examination of texts – although none so adventurous as those advanced by the Dominican, Fr Edmund Hill, in a letter to *The Tablet*, 8 January 1994[41] – and the Anglican understanding of the development of the tradition was expounded. In fact the debate was an excellent illustration of the way in which 'Catholic' and 'Evangelical' complement each other in the quest for catholicity.

As an example of scriptural theology and practice being unfolded in the tradition, we may take the fundamental issue of baptism, by which we become members of Christ, incorporated into his Church. In St Paul's day, although all were seen as equal in Christ, there was yet division as to whether Gentiles could be admitted to baptism. This was settled in Paul's lifetime. The issue of baptised slaves and how their equality should be lived out in the Church was not. It took a little longer. The male-female issue and what their equality in Christ betokens for the Church is before us today. The tradition unfolds, and as Colin Craston said in the debate in General Synod in November 1993,

> The changed personal relationships between men and women established by the Cross can now be more fully reflected both in the social order and in the Church. Why now and not earlier? Because it is only in modern times that the right conditions, the matrix, for this development have come about. It is not a case of the Church being wrong for 2,000 years and us now making a correction. In past generations time was not ripe.

Seen in this way, Anglicanism's unilateral decision is not an impediment to catholicity – though it may delay the progress towards visible unity – but is (to repeat the phrase) an act of eschatological obedience to the future Catholic Church. If indeed it is an insight about the truth of the Gospel that Anglican theology and structures have enabled the Church to perceive and implement in a particular way and at a particular time, then the decision is in itself something which will contribute to the true catholicity of the Church; for it will involve a more intense participation in the divine catholicity – the centre that assures unity.

An ecumenical agenda
Of course we are only at the beginning of the process of discernment in these complex issues. There clearly has to be a continuing exploration of what is

meant, for example, by 'ministerial priesthood', the point raised by Max Thurian. This is examined in *A Fearful Symmetry?*, an interesting discussion paper representing different traditions in the Church, where we read that some scholars in the Roman Catholic Church have recently pointed out that the celebrant is *in persona ecclesiae* prior to being *in persona Christi*. Bernard Cook is quoted as saying in *Ministry of Word and Sacraments*:

> The liturgical celebrant does not offer the sacrifice himself (except insofar as he shares in the community's act of sacrifice), but it is he who makes possible the reciprocal self-giving of Christ and the community, ie. their unified sacrifice. The celebrant does lead the eucharistic assembly as it gives voice to its sacrificial decision, but it is the entire community that corporately professes this decision, and thereby offers sacrifice.[42]

The authors of *A Fearful Symmetry?* go on to say:

> Now [the people of God] can begin to understand that to represent Christ as a priest is not to become in some mystical fashion a latter-day clone of Jesus of Nazareth. They themselves are being called into the priesthood of all believers to represent the crucified and risen Christ who is present now through the Spirit in the Church.[43]

The question then inevitably follows, 'Does God want men and women to exercise together the ministerial priesthood?' Answering in the affirmative, it is striking that the Synod of the Old Catholic Church in Germany committed itself to the ordination of women to the priesthood in 1989, precisely *on the grounds of catholicity*:

> We know ourselves to be called to a catholicity which excludes only everything which undermines the fullness of the relationship of God to his people. Our confession of faith in the Creed, 'We believe in the One, Holy, Catholic and Apostolic Church' obliges us therefore no longer generally to limit the apostolic ministry to the masculine part of the body of the baptized.

It is this kind of question that all the churches together must face. The official conversations between Anglicans and Orthodox, and between Anglicans and Roman Catholics, have not been broken off on account of the question of women's ordination. The authors of *A Fearful Symmetry?* conclude:

> We ourselves as a group, predominantly Orthodox, Roman Catholic and Anglican, have found as we listened to one another and sought to understand one another that our unity was strengthened and deepened. We believe that this experience is not irrelevant to our Churches, and we hope that others of our fellow Church men and women may wish to become involved in a similar process.[44]

Catholicity invites us to partake in this process at every level of the Church's life.

Catholicity and Ecumenism:
from Jerusalem to Porvoo

A Catholic Anglican development?

The affair of the Jerusalem bishopric (see page 8) was perceived by the Tractarians to offend Catholic order. Can Catholic Anglicans today properly be involved in the kind of exploration suggested by the group who produced *A Fearful Symmetry?* George Guiver CR of Mirfield has argued that tradition is properly understood as 'momentum', a moving forward, as it were, of the past into the present.[45] This is the path we are walking in and in this particular instance there is a bridge from the past.

In his book *The Olive Branch: an Evangelical Anglican Doctrine of the Church,*[46] Tim Bradshaw says that 'the Anglo-Catholic theory of episcopal Church order has been shown, by Newbigin especially, to place the Church below the ministry, to legitimate episcopal schism in the name of catholicity, and to reject visible union with other world-wide churches while at the same time acknowledging that they are indwelt by the Holy Spirit.'

It would be more accurate to say that this was *an* influential Anglo-Catholic theory rather than *the* Anglo-Catholic theory. Certainly such a theory lies at the heart of John Jay Hughes' argument, which was criticised by Roman Catholics precisely because it inverts the position of Church and Ministry. Another expression showing the absurdity of the position is in *episcopi vagentes,* who have valid orders (in the tactile sense) but no community from which they emerge. It was on the lack of such validity of orders that much Anglo-Catholic opposition focused at the birth of the Church of South India.

However, there is another Catholic Anglican tradition that has avoided this trap, and it is well expressed in the writings of Father Herbert Kelly, Founder of the Society of the Sacred Mission, which sponsored one of the largest Catholic theological colleges in the Church of England from the end of the nineteenth century until 1971, and was responsible for work in theological education in other parts of the communion, notably Australia, Southern Africa and Ghana.

With Frere from Mirfield and a delegation from SPG, Father Kelly was present at the Edinburgh Missionary Conference of 1910. They were unusual figures at this largely Protestant ecumenical gathering, but Kelly's presence was not an eccentric diversion. It was part of his understanding of the nature of catholicity that Catholic Anglicans should be in the forefront of ecumenical dialogue, not only with Rome, but with the Protestant Churches of the Reformation. His criticism of the Catholic *party* (and indeed of the Church of England as a whole) arose from precisely that inversion of the place of the ministry in relation to the Church to which Bradshaw objects.

Writing from Japan in 1916, Kelly emphasised that the Church had problems because it had got the relationship between Church and ministry the wrong way round.

> In our practice today the Church is almost entirely dependent on the clergy. The Church in a parish consists of all those people that the clergy can persuade to take an interest in religion. If the clergy possess the rare gift of influence – without which holiness and self-sacrifice effect little – things go well. If a Vicar without gifts follows a Vicar with gifts, everything seems to come to a standstill. We are so accustomed to this way of thinking and working that it never occurs to us that there is or could be any other, although in fact our way is peculiarly Anglican. We do not observe that for the old Creed, 'I believe in the Holy Catholic Church', we are mentally substituting a new clause, 'I believe in holy and energetic clergy'.[47]

This is the Creed of clericalism. Kelly believed that Anglicans had things to learn about the Church and ministry from what he called 'the denominations'. In his book *Catholicity* he comments on his involvement with the ecumenical movement and with those from the Catholic party of the Church of England who had joined with him in it.

> What was new in the desire for a Catholic unity was the spirit of self-criticism, the sense that whatever we had gained, there were things we were missing, and that we had a real need of one another. Anglicans felt it much more than they were wont to do; all religious bodies in England and Scotland felt it; the Lutheran Churches in Germany, Sweden, Denmark, showed it more than any . . . They were beginning to be conscious that the Christian faith meant a great deal more than any one body can by itself realise.[48]

It was this spirit that allowed the Society of the Sacred Mission to be the only one of the Anglo-Catholic communities not to oppose the South India Scheme in 1947. It was a sign of the times as 'party' diminished and the realisation of its Catholic identity became part of the heritage of the whole *ecclesia anglicana*.

So we see that within what we may now call the Catholic Anglican tradition there has been a development of its ecclesiology faithful to Hooker and the Caroline Divines. The Church, the mystical body, is both triumphant in heaven and militant here on earth. In its visible form it has a sacramental ministry, historically evolved and subordinate to the Church – and under the authority of the Gospel. Can Catholics go on to say that what validates the ministry is its faithfulness to the Gospel task, of which the tactile succession is the sacramental sign but not the substance?

The Porvoo Agenda
In 1992 a common statement was issued following continuing conversations between the British and Irish Anglican Churches and the Nordic and Baltic Lutheran Churches. It is the culmination of a process that began in 1909, but it is particularly significant in the new climate of theological debate which was given momentum by the Lutheran Episcopal Agreement of 1982 in the United States of America, and by the Meissen Common Statement of 1988 between the Church of England and the Evangelical Churches in East and West Germany. These agreements led to 'mutual eucharistic hospitality, a limited degree of sharing ordained ministry, occasional joint celebrations of the Eucharist and a commitment to common life and mission'.[49]

The Porvoo Statement begins with the acknowledgement of 'one another's churches as churches belonging to the One, Holy, Catholic and Apostolic Church of Jesus Christ', where the Word of God is authentically preached and the sacraments administered on the basis of sharing in the common confession of the apostolic faith.

It also states:

> We acknowledge that one another's ordained ministries are given by God as instruments of his grace and as possessing not only the inward call of the Spirit, but also Christ's commission through his body, the Church;
> we acknowledge that personal, collegial and communal oversight (*episcope*) is embodied and exercised in all our churches in a variety of forms, in continuity of apostolic life, mission and ministry;
> we acknowledge that the episcopal office is valued and maintained in all our churches as a visible sign expressing and serving the Church's unity and continuity in apostolic life, mission and ministry.[50]

The Statement proposes that the churches commit themselves to a mutual recognition of ministries and 'to invite one another's bishops normally to participate in the laying on of hands at the ordination of bishops as a sign of the unity and continuity of the Church'.

In a carefully argued historical study of Orders and Ordination in Denmark, Norway and Iceland, John Halliburton notes that it is quite clear that the intention of the rites of these churches 'is to continue and ordain to the ministry a pastoral and spiritual oversight which from apostolic times has been the task of the bishop',[51] and that all the essential and traditional elements of a rite of Ordination in the Western Church are present. In the tradition of Catholic Anglicanism to which I have referred, the Porvoo

Statement offers a significant way forward in the search for the recovery of the principles of catholicity in Northern Europe.

To these conversations, Anglicans have brought their own special theology and tradition, and have been able to offer them in a way that may enhance the continuing dialogue with Rome. But Anglicans are not simply 'enablers'. Such conversations matter to us because if we do not pay attention to our catholicity we shall become an eccentric irrelevance. In the nineteenth century danger was perceived in the way the State could interfere with and distort the Church's catholicity. Today, Anglicans are conscious of being marginalised by the State, and of the Church becoming an institution to which the majority of people are indifferent. We have to ensure that our Order is directed to fulfil the Gospel task at home as well as contributing to the dialogue with other churches, including the nonconformist churches of the United Kingdom.

Recently a radio commentator remarked, *à propos* of the conversion to Rome of the Duchess of Kent, that he could not imagine anyone converting to the Church of England unless it was because he had in some way offended the discipline of the Roman Church and conversion was therefore 'convenient'. The speaker was not being particularly aggressive or unpleasant, but clearly had no idea of the kind of church that Anglicans belong to. Perhaps one cannot properly evaluate any church unless one has been part of it, spiritually nourished in its fellowship and shaped by its common worship. Those of us who have mourned and celebrated through its rituals, struggled in the faith through the resources of its theology, and been pastored through its ministry rejoice in the Church of England and think our time well spent, as Stillingfleet said, 'defending its cause'. But Catholic Anglicans do this knowing that the cause includes a commitment to unity that is based on the development of those essentials that enable it to be 'turned towards the centre' – Christ, who is All in all. Herein lies our catholicity.

Notes

1 Edward Stillingfleet, *A Discourse concerning the Idolatry practised in the Church of Rome*, 1676.

2 *The Ordination of Women to the Priesthood: the Synod Debate, 11 November 1992*, London, Church House Publishing 1993.

3 Henri de Lubac, *The Motherhood of the Church*, San Francisco, Ignatius Press 1982.

4 Cited G. R. Elton, *The Tudor Constitution: documents and commentary*, Cambridge, Cambridge University Press 1972, pp. 356ff.

5 Paul Avis, *The Church in the Theology of the Reformers*, London, Marshall's Theological Library 1981, p. 161.

6 Second Vatican Council, *Schema constitutionis dogmaticae de ecclesia*, Vatican City 1963, Chapter 1.

7 Cited Avis, op. cit.

8 John Jewel, *Works*, Cambridge, Parker Society 1848–50, Part 4, p. 668.

9 Richard Hooker, *Apologia Ecclesiae Anglicanae*.

10 'The Laws of Ecclesiastical Polity', III.i.14, in *The Works of Richard Hooker*, Vol. 1, ed. John Keble, Oxford, Oxford University Press 1888.

11 Ibid.

12 Ibid.

13 T. S. Eliot, 'The Hippopotamus' in *Complete Poems 1909–1935*, London, Faber & Faber 1936, p. 50.

14 Diarmaid MacCulloch, 'The Myth of the English Reformation' in *History Today*, July 1991.

15 J. H. Newman, 'Sermon on the Communion of Saints' at St Mary's, Oxford, May 1835.

16 Both rely on St Augustine, *De Civitate Dei*.

17 William Palmer, *Treatise on the Church of Christ*, 2 volumes, London 1838.

18 John Jay Hughes, *Epistola ad Fratrem Anglicanum*, *The Tablet*, 5 June 1993.

19   Letter to F. W. Newman, 10 November 1840, cited in J. Tolhurst, *The Church – a Communion*, Leominster, Fowler Wright 1988.

20   Letter to Archdeacon Manning, 25 October 1843.

21   André Lascaris OP, in a paper entitled 'A Moral Heart for Europe', read in the Department of Continuing Education of the University of Oxford, 17 March 1993.

22   The Lambeth Conference 1948, *The Encyclical Letter from the Bishops: together with Resolutions and Report*, London SPCK 1948, pp. 84–86.

23   1st Lambeth Conference 1867.

24   I am greatly indebted to Mark Chapman for allowing me to read two unpublished papers, 'Truro and Carthage: Archbishop Benson and the Unity of the Church' and 'Catholicity, Unity and Provincial Autonomy: on making decisions unilaterally', to be published in a shortened form in *The Anglican Theological Review* as 'Catholicity, Unity and Provincial Autonomy: on making decisions unilaterally', summer 1994. Mark Chapman is Lecturer in Systematic Theology at Ripon College, Cuddesdon.

25   Lewis Carroll, *Through the Looking Glass*, first published London, Macmillan 1871.

26   Aidan Nichol OP, *Holy Order*, Dublin, Veritas Press 1990.

27   *Church of England Newspaper*, 28 May 1993.

28   *Belonging Together*, Inter-Anglican Theological Doctrinal Consultation 1992.

29   'Unity within the Anglican Communion', Opening Address to the Lambeth Conference 1988, cited in Adrian Hastings, *Robert Runcie*, London, Mowbray 1991.

30   ARCIC – the Final Report of the Anglican Roman Catholic International Commission – was published in 1982.

31   Statement of Roman Catholic Bishops' Conference of England and Wales, 23 April 1993.

32   Letter from Pope John Paul II to Archbishop Robert Runcie, 20 December 1984.

33   Report of Archbishops' Commission on Women and Holy Orders, 1963.

34   Letter from Archbishop Robert Runcie to Pope John Paul II, 11 December 1985.

35   Stephen Sykes, *The Identity of Christianity: theologians and the essence of Christianity from Schleiermacher to Barth*, London, SPCK 1984, p. 285.

36   Report of the Archbishops' Commission on Communion and Women in the Episcopate, 1989 (The Eames Commission).

37   *Episcopal Ministry*, the Report of the Archbishops' Group on the Episcopate, London, Church House Publishing 1990.

38   It had been discussed since 1960, when the Church in Sweden put it on the ecumenical agenda.

39   *Catholic Herald*, 2 April 1993.

40   *Centro* – News from the Anglican Centre in Rome, April 1993.

41   He refers, for example, to Phoebe (*diakonon*), Priscilla (possibly a *presbutera* or even an *episkopos*) of the church in their house. He concludes: 'I submit that on the one hand the New Testament provides no basis for the ordination of anyone, male or female, in the sense of *sacerdos*; while it does provide some evidence for the existence of women as well as men in the rank of priest as *presbuteros* or *presbuter*'. *Presbutera* continues to appear in the Church during the subsequent four centuries.

42   *A Fearful Symmetry? The Complementarity of Men and Women in Ministry*, A. M. Allchin and others, with a foreword by John V. Taylor, London, SPCK 1992, pp. 46–7.

43   Ibid. p. 47.

44   Ibid. p. 53.

45   George Guiver CR, *Faith in Momentum*, London, SPCK 1990.

46   Tim Bradshaw, *The Olive Branch: an Evangelical Anglican Doctrine of the Church*, Exeter, Paternoster Press 1992.

47   *East and West*, a quarterly review for the study of missionary problems, London 1916.

48   Herbert Kelly SSM, *Catholicity*, London, SCM Press 1932.

49   *Together in Mission and Ministry*, The Porvoo Common Statement, London, Church House Publishing 1993, p. 2.

50   Ibid. p. 30.

51   John Halliburton, in an essay in *Together in Mission and Ministry*.